Prof(
Wisdom
of
The Heart Sutra
and Other Teachings

Profound Wisdom of The Heart Sutra

and Other Teachings

Bokar Rinpoche
Kenpo Donyo

Translation from Tibetan into French
Tashi Oser
François Jacquemart
Rinchen Tsomo

English Translation
Christiane Buchet

ClearPoint Press
San Francisco, California

Profound Wisdom of the Heart Sutra
and Other Teachings

Published by:

ClearPoint Press

PO Box 170658

San Francisco, CA 94117

The original text of this book was published in French and was titled **Profondeur de la Sagesse**.

Copyright reserved for all countries:

Association Claire Lumière

5 avenue Camille Pelletan

13760 St Cannat, France.

Copyright ©1994 English Edition

ClearPoint Press

Printed in the United States of America

Book printed on acid-free paper

Second Printing 2002

Library of Congress Catalog Card Number: 94-68742

ISBN 0-9630371-3-7

Prajnaparamita Cover Drawing: Cynthia Moku

Introduction

The reader of this book will discover three different and complementary teachings. First of all, a literal translation of the Heart Sutra followed by a commentary.

Perhaps the best known piece of literature expounding the Buddha's teachings, the Heart Sutra is read and chanted by most of the Mahayana schools (Great Vehicle). Within the teachings of Prajnaparamita (the Mother of all Buddhas), it is defined as the heart or essence of these teachings, as suggested by its title. When we enter the path of Prajnaparamita, we soon discover that our biggest problem is that we see reality through the distortions created by our own mind. How can we approach outer and inner phenomena in a better way? This is precisely the subject of the Heart Sutra. Of course, this is not easy. Bokar Rinpoche offers a thorough explanation of the text in order to open and broaden our understanding. His teachings go further allowing us to taste the ultimate realization of Transcendent Wisdom, and showing us the nonreality of phenomena.

This instruction was delivered by Bokar Rinpoche on his first visit to Europe in 1980. Transcribed and orally translated by Venerable Tashi Oser, the text was then published by *Les Cahiers du Bouddhisme* in June and October 1984. We have translated into English the edited French version of Lama Chöky (François Jacquemart) published by *Claire Lumière* in 1986. In the commentary part, the quotes of the literal translation are set in bold type, while italics indicate a slightly different version given during the oral teaching.

As a further help, Bokar Rinpoche gives a second teaching entitled "Concerning Anger." He shows another distorted view of reality—anger. To rid ourselves of it, Bokar Rinpoche stresses the instrumental power of love and compassion inseparable from the wisdom exposed in the Heart Sutra commentary. This teaching was given on September 1985, in Montpellier, France. The last chapter is the teaching of Khenpo Donyo. After completing long studies of Buddhism culminating in a Doctorate degree, he became Bokar Rinpoche's main disciple always accompanying Bokar Rinpoche on his tours. Khenpo Donyo is famous for his erudition and gentle manner in clearly exposing Buddhist concepts. His topic on karma was expounded in Aix en Provence, France, in 1985. This is a final guide on the path for looking at phenomena, in accordance with the law of karma. In this way, we learn that responsibility for our sorrows and happiness belongs to us alone.

This book is the result of the efforts of several people. We are profoundly grateful to Bokar Rinpoche for these precious teachings filled with wisdom, love and compassion, and to Khenpo Donyo for his clarity in explaining karma. We are indebted to Lama Chöky (François Jacquemart) for the French version translated with the help of Tashi Oser and Rinchen Tsomo. Many generous friends helped in the different phases of the production. Thanks to Chiao and Ernie Crews, Michael De Noya, Hubert Godard, Juanita Hall, Don Iocca, Gene Meyer, Bill Minassian, William Sleeper, and Isao Tanaka for their love and support. Special thanks are due to Karen Graham who worked on the cover and proofread the text. Chen-Jer Jan did the layout of the book and offered his computer expertise. Elson Snow read the first draft of the manuscript bringing many improvements. Rosemary Gilpin patiently read the entire text offering encouragement.

May the reading of this book bring you wisdom and happiness!

Table Of Content

The Heart Sutra

Bhagavati Prajna Paramita Hridaya
Heart of the Great Perfection of Transcendent Wisdom
Homage to the Noble Lady, the Perfection of Transcendent Wisdom.

Thus have I heard these words.[1] Once the Blessed One[2] was dwelling in Rajagriha at Vulture Peak,[3] together with a great gathering of monks and bodhisattvas.[4] At that time the Blessed Lord entered the samadhi that expresses phenomena called *profound illumination.*

At the same time, the Noble Avalokiteshvara,[5] the *bodhisattva-mahasattva*, observed carefully the practice of the profound Perfection of Transcendent Wisdom. He saw precisely that the five aggregates[6] were themselves empty by nature.

Through the power of the inspiration of the Buddha, venerable Shariputra[7] said to the Noble Avalokiteshvara, the *bodhisattva-mahasattva:*

"How should a son or a daughter of noble family[8] train, who wishes to practice the Profound Perfection of Transcendent Wisdom?"

Addressed in this manner, the Noble Avalokiteshvara answered the venerable Shariputra.

"O, Shariputra, a son or daughter of noble family who wishes to practice the Profound Perfection of Transcendent Wisdom should see it like this:

The five aggregates themselves are empty by nature. One should see that in a precise and pure way. Form is emptiness. Emptiness is form. Emptiness is no other than form; form is no other than emptiness. In the same way, feelings, perceptions, mental formations, and consciousnesses[9] are empty.

Thus, Shariputra, all phenomena are empty; they have no characteristics, no origin, no cessation, no impurity, no purity, no decrease, no wholeness.

Thus, Shariputra, in emptiness, there is no form, no feeling, no perception, no mental formation, no consciousness.[10]

There is no eye, no ear, no nose, no tongue, no body, no mind.[11]

There is no appearance, no sound, no smell, no taste, no touch, no phenomena.[12]

There is no visual constituent and so on up to no mental constituent and no mental consciousness constituent.[13]

There is no ignorance, no cessation of ignorance and so on up to no old age and death, no cessation of old age and death.[14]

Likewise, there is no suffering, no origin of suffering, no cessation of suffering, no path.[15]

There is no primordial awareness, no accomplishment, and no nonaccomplishment.

Therefore, Shariputra, because the bodhisattvas have nothing to attain, they leave it up to the Profound Perfection of Transcendent Wisdom and dwell in it. Their minds being without veil, they have no fear. Having reached beyond any error, they have attained the state beyond suffering.

All the Buddhas manifesting in the three times,[16] effectively have attained the totally pure, unsurpassable, and perfect Awakening by leaving it up to this Profound Transcendent Wisdom.

Therefore, the mantra of Transcendent Wisdom, the mantra of great insight, the unsurpassable mantra, the mantra that equals the unequaled, the mantra that perfectly dissipates all suffering should be known as Truth since there is no falsehood. The mantra of the Perfection of Transcendent Wisdom[17] is said like this:

Tayata om gate gate paragate para samgate bodhi soha

Thus, Shariputra, it is in this manner that the *bodhisattva-mahasattva* should train in the Profound Perfection of Transcendent Wisdom."

Then the Blessed One arose from that samadhi and approved the word of the Noble Avalokiteshvara, the *bodhisattva-mahasattva*, saying, "Good, good, O son of noble family, thus it is, thus it really is. One should practice the Profound Perfection of Transcendent Wisdom just as you have expounded it. The Tathagatas,[18] themselves rejoice."

When the Blessed One had said this, venerable Shariputra and Noble Avalokiteshvara, the *bodhisattva-mahasattva*, all those who were in the assembly as well as the world of the *devas*, humans, *asuras* and *gandharvas*,[19] rejoiced and praised the words of the Blessed One.

1. The Buddha has not written a word. Sutras that collect his words were retold from memory and written by his principal disciples, in particular, Ananda, when they gathered in a council one year after his *parinirvana*. Sutras always start with a sentence reminding us of this fact.

2. This designates the Buddha.

3. Vulture Peak, near Rajagriha in the Magadha area, was the place chosen by the Buddha to transmit most of the *Mahayana*, particularly the *Prajnaparamita* teachings.

4. The bodhisattvas belong to the *Mahayana*. They are all those on the path of Awakening who cultivate the motivation of benefiting others. However, this term often refers to those who, already liberated of samsara but having not yet attained complete Awakening, dwell in the ten *bhumis* or ten Bodhisattvas levels.

5. Tibetan, Chenrezig.

6. The five aggregates are forms, feelings, perceptions, mental formations, and consciousnesses.

7. Shariputra is one of the eighty great disciples of the Buddha. He is famous for his particular ability with the abhidharma. The fact that Shariputra's question has for consequence the Heart Sutra utterance, shows that the content of this sutra begins where abhidharma ends.

8. A son or a daughter of noble family is a member of the *Mahayana* family.

9. The exact term would be "dichotomous consciousness" or "individualized consciousness"; in other words, it functions in the dualistic division between subject and object. One traditionally counts six consciousnesses, corresponding as inner receptors to the six sense organs and their objects: visual, auditory, olfactory, gustatory, tactile, and mental consciousness.

Sometimes one adds two other consciousnesses: disturbed consciousness and potential of consciousness. It is necessary to understand that the term "potential of consciousness" does not refer here to the dualistic individualized consciousness that is a defective functioning of the mind. When the mind is pure, one talks then of primordial nondual awareness.

10. The five aggregates are negated here.

11. The six sense organs are negated here.

12. The six sense objects are negated: here, phenomena are objects of mental sense.

13. The eighteen constituents are negated:
   - six sense objects
   - six sense organs
   - six consciousnesses

14. In parallel, the twelve interdependent factors are negated: ignorance, karmic formations, individual consciousness, name and form, six senses, contact, sensation, craving, grasping, becoming, birth, old age, and death, as well as exhaustion of each of them.

15. The four Noble Truths are negated.

16. Past, present, and future.

17. See the meaning of the mantra in Bokar Rinpoche's explanation. We give here the Tibetan pronunciation of the mantra. It is slightly different in its Sanskrit pronunciation.

18. Tathagata is another word to designate a Buddha. Literally, it means the one who is gone into the suchness.

19. *Gandharvas* are celestial musician spirits feeding on smells, similar to the muses.

Part I

The one who has perfectly abandoned that which should have been abandoned, the one who has perfectly accomplished that which should have been accomplished, the Perfect Buddha, has given this teaching with the unique goal of helping all beings, that is to say, ourselves.

This teaching does not exhaust the supreme wisdom of the Buddha, which embraces all dharmas,[1] whatever they are. The Buddha's teaching is exactly proportional to the needs of those who listen to it. It does not constitute the totality of his supreme wisdom, but this portion has been truly used to discipline beings who have addressed him.

Beings, prisoners in the cycle of conditioned existence (samsara), live in illusion, perceiving that which is not existing as existing. This particularly concerns the I/me. They also perceive as permanent and eternal that which is impermanent, and perceive as happiness that which is in fact suffering.

The egocentric grasping (experience of feeling me) is innate. A child in the cradle feels it spontaneously. Outer phenomena are essentially transitory. They do not have any permanence and pass from instant to instant without any real stability. However, we grasp them as stable, remaining, permanent, and this is not a learned experience. Joy and happiness in the cycle of existence are themselves causes of suffering. However, we grasp only their pleasant aspects. This does not require any apprenticeship, either.

There are things that one naturally considers as impure and unclean. Generally, human beings attach this feeling to feces. Although these impure matters are coming directly out of the body, we consider this body perfectly clean and pure.

In this way the fourfold grasping of phenomena is manifested:
- the I/me
- permanence
- happiness
- purity

These are the four notions inherent to our relationships with the cycle of existence.

If the Buddha had directly addressed people, affirming, "There is no me, all phenomena are impermanent, all is suffering, all is impure," perhaps he would have aroused a vague nod of approval within the most respectful of his listeners (if he says so, it is certainly true). At the least, it would have been difficult to make them directly perceive the truth of these observations. More than likely, he would have engendered serious doubts about his mental health.

- Why?

The listener would have thought, I am perfectly happy, who affirms that I am not?

- I, so scrupulously clean; who tells me that I am unclean and impure!

- I, myself; who tells me that I am not!

The Buddha gave his teachings gradually. The first time, he turned the wheel of the teachings at Benares in

India, for an audience that included his five first disciples.[2] He transmitted, at that time, the teaching concerned with the four noble truths.[3] He taught that what is called me, is, in reality, composed of five aggregates (skandhas): form, feeling, perception, mental formation, and consciousness. He showed that what we called I/me, that which seems to be a monolithic entity, one, is in fact a multiple reality. The egocentric grasping of an I is, in fact, the grasping of five aggregates, the grasping of not a simple but a fivefold phenomenon.

Most of us, when we say I/me, do not think about what we are saying. We consider it as obvious.

- I, well ... it is me!

But first, the Buddha made his listeners realize that I/me was not as simple as it appeared and that I/me was composed of the five aggregates.

- The first aggregate, the aggregate of form, is constituted by the union of the five elements: earth, water, fire, air, and space.

- The second one, the aggregate of feeling, is related to form. Three kinds of feelings are distinguished: pleasant, unpleasant, or neutral.

- The third is the aggregate of perception. There are two types:

• pure perception, which corresponds to reality: perceptions of phenomena and their interrelationships as they really are.

• impure perception, characterized by a mode of illusory functioning, which does not correspond to the phenomena as they are.

- The fourth one is the aggregate of mental formations. There are three types: one linked to the body, one to speech, and one to the mind.

- The fifth one is the consciousness aggregate, that is to say, the mind aware of the appearances.

All this in its multiplicity is what we call I/me.

All that remains, all that is not me, can be perceived through the eighteen fields of extension of the senses, or more exactly, the six threefold fields of extension of the senses.

- visual sense, which processes forms, colors, and so on
- auditory sense, which processes sounds
- olfactory sense, which processes smells
- gustatory sense, which processes tastes
- tactile sense, which processes objects of touch
- mental sense, which processes impressions, mental formations, and images that follow them

These senses correspond to the six consciousnesses in which they manifest:

- Visual, auditory, olfactory, gustatory, tactile, and mental consciousnesses as well as the six objects that they are intended to apprehend: forms, smells, tastes, sounds, objects of touch, and mental objects (Tibetan, cho; Sanskrit, dharma), which belong to the mental domain.

The six senses, six objects, and six consciousnesses form the eighteen elements of the senses.

When the Buddha started the first cycle of teaching, he stressed and showed that the so-called I/me and the feelings that feed it are not simple. He showed that what we consider our obvious reality on no way corresponds to the monolithic conception we have of it. The I/me is a group of five aggregates that enters a relationship with an outer world (which is not me) through the eighteen sense elements.

Then, the Buddha showed how action evolves from these phenomena. He also revealed how some actions lead to suffering and others to happiness. Clearly explaining the law of causality (karma), he exhorted those listening to him to abstain from the ten negative acts[4] and practice the ten virtuous acts. This established ethics based on a clear understanding of its necessity.

After having brought his disciples to the right livelihood indispensable for a sane spiritual practice, the Buddha turned the Wheel of the Teachings for the second time at Rajagriha on Vulture Peak for an audience of bodhisattvas. He then taught the absence of characteristics.

This teaching of the Great Mother (Tibetan, Yum Chenmo), the mother of all Buddhas, *Prajnaparamita*, consists of twelve volumes in its extensive version, seven in its average version, and one in its most concise version. The essence, the core of his teaching of *Prajnaparamita*, the Virtue of Transcendent Wisdom, is enunciated in the Heart

Sutra of Transcendent Wisdom (Prajnaparamita Hridaya Sutra) that we now are going to study.

The original text, written in Sanskrit, the most noble of the four great languages of India, is entitled **Bhagavati Prajna Paramita Hridaya**, rendered in Tibetan by Chomdendema Sherab Ki Paroltushinpay Nyingpo, the Heart of the Victorious Transcendent Wisdom.

Bhaga: Victorious (Tibetan, chom). Victorious One over the four kinds of demons that we carry within us. Following our egocentric grasping, they are:

- demon of the aggregates
- demon of self-satisfaction or happiness
- demon of death
- demon of conflicting emotions

Vati: Endowed with (Tibetan, den) and beyond (Tibetan, dema). Endowed with all qualities and beyond the cycle of conditioned existence.

Prajna: Wisdom (Tibetan, sherab).

Paramita: Gone beyond (Tibetan, paroltushinpa). That is to say, knowledge of the true nature of this wisdom allows one to go "beyond."

Hridaya: Heart (Tibetan, nyingpo). In front of this gathering of bodhisattvas, the Buddha enunciated the essence of this Transcendent Wisdom.

Some translations begin with an invocation:

Homage to the Victorious Transcendent Wisdom, a short prayer from the Tibetan translator who places himself under the aegis of *Prajnaparamita*.

**Thus have I heard these words. Once the Blessed One
was dwelling at Vulture Peak.** These words reveal and summarize the text to follow,
and show the five perfections.

Dike: This word. Summarizing all which will be said later,
the phrase "this word" indicates that in its perfection the
text contains all the Transcendent Wisdom, the Dharma,
the excellent teaching.

Da ki: By me. Designates those who have heard this word
when it was told. They are the bodhisattvas gathered
around the Buddha.

Tu Chik na: In one instant, a moment. This refers to the
perfect moment, the eminently right moment.

Chom den de: The Bhagavat, the Buddha. It is the Perfect
Teacher.

Gyal po kap ja go pung po ri la: In the royal domain
called the Mountain Where the Vultures Gather. It is the
perfect place for the revelation of Wisdom.

This first verse exposes:

- the subject: this word. *Prajnaparamita*
- the listener: assembly of bodhisattvas
- the time: in this perfect and right moment
- the teacher: the Buddha himself
- the place: Vulture Peak

*While a great number of monks and perfect bodhisattvas
gathered, the Victorious One dwelled in meditative absorption
during which he perceived the profound characteristics of
phenomena; this meditation is called profound illumination.*

This indicates one of the many possible forms of samadhi where the Buddha was.

At the same time, the Noble Avalokiteshvara, the *bodhisattva-mahasattva* **observed carefully the practice of the Profound Perfection of Transcendent Wisdom. He precisely saw that the five aggregates were empty by nature.**

Many kinds of teachings or words of the Buddha exist:
- words spoken by the Buddha himself
- teachings transmitted by the Buddha by means of the light emitted by his crown protrusion
- finally, a teaching given by someone and made possible by the grace conferred by the Buddha

By the grace of the Buddha, the bodhisattva Avalokiteshvara (Chenrezig) dwelled in the meditative absorption where he was perceiving the profound meaning of the Transcendent Wisdom.

Chenrezig, although not being a perfectly realized Buddha, had access to the perfect and unveiled knowledge of the Buddha through this grace.

Through the power of the inspiration of the Buddha, venerable Shariputra said to the Noble Avalokiteshvara... Because of the fact of this grace—somehow inciting—Shariputra found himself pressured to ask Chenrezig for an explanation of what he was perceiving.

How should a son or a daughter of noble family train, who wishes to practice the Profound Perfection of Transcendent Wisdom?

The Noble Chenrezig (Arya Avalokiteshvara) responded:

A son or a daughter of noble family who wishes to understand the profound meaning of the Transcendent Wisdom should see it like this: the five aggregates are empty by nature.

We already have seen that, during the first turning of the wheel of the dharma, the Buddha began by teaching that me was only the union of five aggregates. Among these aggregates, the aggregate of form exists only by the combination of the five elements: earth, water, fire, air, and space. Outside these five elements, the aggregate of form does not exist; therefore, it is empty (of its own existence).

Perhaps, one will object, it is composed of elements that exist by themselves. Let us examine them.

The earth element, as it concerns us, corresponds to the skeleton of our body and the flesh enveloping it. This material may be divided, cut into parts more and more numerous until, theoretically, one obtains a base particle, nondivisible, noncompounded, an atom (Greek, a-tomos). However, to logically exist, this atom itself must be determined spatially. That is, it must have a front, back, above, underneath, right, and left. Lacking these parameters, it would not belong to our spatial reference system and would have no existence for us. However, if such a particle is integrated in such a reference system, this implies that a part of it is on top, another at the bottom, and so on. Having such parts, it is no longer indivisible (a-tomos); it would not be this *constitutive brick* of all matter. One can repeat this ad infinitum. The logical conclusion of this operation is the nonexistence of such a base particle, material and indivisible, from which different elements could be made up, and whose coalescence forms physical matter under its multiple aspects. The earth element, then, can be considered as empty (of its own existence). The same logical process, adapted and applied to each of the elements, allows the demonstration of their emptiness, their nonexistence, at least as one usually understands it. One arrives at the conclusion that the aggregate of form is empty.

Let us now see the second aggregate, feeling.

The range of feelings can be divided in three categories: pleasant, unpleasant, and neutral.

By applying a precise analytical method, for example, to the pleasant side of the aggregate of feeling, one shows the nonexistence of this *joy* or *pleasure* as an intrinsic entity. One continues then with the other two categories of feeling to arrive at the negation of existence of the aggregate in its totality.

By similar examination of the aggregate of perception, one sees that perceptions (the recognition of a sense or mental object as having some characteristics: red, round, squared, and so on) are without own existence, showing the emptiness of the aggregate in its totality.

This analytical method is worth considering.

- perception: it is red.

What is necessary for the appearance of this perception of red?

- First, a red object,

- perceived by the means of an instrument, the sense organ of sight,

- this perception by the sense organ is integrated in the sense consciousness,

- the sense consciousness itself is received in the reservoir consciousness

- then it is analyzed by the mental consciousness, and so on.

It is necessary to use at least five elements in order to obtain the perception red, which in itself is lacking intrinsic existence.

One will then proceed to analyse the aggregate of mental formation by reducing it through logical examination to its intrinsic nonexistence.

The aggregate of consciousness will be recognized as not indivisible, not monolithic, but as being sixfold, composed of six parts—visual, auditory, gustatory, olfactory, tactile, and mental consciousnesses. Examination of each one of them allows for a demonstration of its nonexistence as an intrinsic entity.

The Buddha says to the noble assembly, *"the five aggregates are empty by nature."* That is, they are not made empty, did not become empty, were not emptied. They are empty by their own nature. Their nature is emptiness. This implies that this emptiness of the aggregates is not a resulting emptiness like that in the case of the aggregate of form. To show emptiness in the aggregate of form, one takes a form and mentally cuts it infinitely. One arrives, then, at a logical absurdity, at a nothing-at-all that is the result of the process of division.

Form is emptiness.

This refers here to the essential impermanent characteristic of form, to the fact that no form lasts or exists in itself. However, as we have seen, one of the fundamental characteristics of the ordinary individual is the grasping of phenomena as permanent and continuous. It is this grasping that produces what is called form.

Emptiness is form.

This second affirmation, immediately following the first one, confirms that *form* and *emptiness* are not antinomic; instead of excluding each other, they are one and the same reality.

There is no other emptiness than form,
there is no other form than emptiness.

Forms, as phenomena that we perceive are empty (of own existence), and it is our grasping of them as *"being"* that makes us perceive them as really existing.

Feeling is emptiness,
emptiness is feeling,
there is no other emptiness than feeling,
there is no other feeling than emptiness.

Perception is emptiness,
emptiness is perception,
There is no other emptiness than perception,
there is no other perception than emptiness.

Mental formation is emptiness,
emptiness is mental formation,
there is no other emptiness than mental formation,
there is no other mental formation than emptiness.

Consciousness is emptiness,
emptiness is consciousness,
there is no other emptiness than consciousness,
there is no other consciousness than emptiness.

Such is the enunciation of the emptiness of the five aggregates. Of course, it is necessary to understand what this enunciation means. Trying to arrive at this understanding, we conceive a vague idea of what it is in matter, but we do not clearly perceive the reality covering these concepts. To perceive this reality, it is necessary to experience it in meditation. Through this method, real understanding can come. It is then a realization-experiencing-consciousness of that which is apprehended, directly, clearly and beyond the veils of the words.

ko wa, nyam nyong, tok pa: understanding, experience, realization.

If we look through a window and see something distant approaching us, we will, first of all, see a black dot without immediately distinguishing what it is. This is **ko wa,** understanding.

Through more careful examination, as the object gets closer, we will figure out a certain amount of characteristics and we will become aware that the object is a man. This second step corresponds to **nyam nyong,** experiencing.

As this man approaches us, we will recognize a friend and rejoice. Our perplexity has disappeared. This is realization, **tok pa.**

The process is the same for the *Prajnaparamita;* while the intellectual understanding holds us very far from it, the experience brings us closer to the point where we realize it. **Thus, Shariputra, all phenomena are empty.**

Having considered the emptiness of the five aggregates, we can affirm that all phenomena—objects of knowledge, or dharmas—are empty. If they are examined, we see they are lacking origin (although they appear to have a beginning). There is no base from which they can appear. The phrase "lacking origin" should be understood with the temporal meaning of no beginning, and no own substance.

If we examine an emotion, for instance, anger, we become aware that it exists with no factual base from which this anger can arise or have existence.

The mental phenomenon, anger, is then going to cease. This implies that this energy will be absorbed in something. However, deeper examination shows the nonexistence of such a place of absorption. This leads to the affirmation that phenomena are devoid of cessation.

They are also without impurity. The mind, in its ultimate reality, is emptiness. It is the basis for all phenomena; it is devoid of characteristic, similar to space, and cannot be soiled. Not being soiled, the dharmas are not liberated from impurity. Being empty, lacking an own existence, they are without decrease; they are not decreasing, neither can they increase. Being from the beginning lacking in qualities and characteristics, there is nothing in the dharmas themselves that can be increased. If one adds nothing to nothing, one obtains nothing. Therefore, they are without increase.

Thus Shariputra, in emptiness there is no form, no feeling, no perception, no mental formation, and no consciousness.

The five aggregates being devoid of their own nature, so it is for the eighteen elements.

There is no eye, no ear, no nose, no tongue, no body, no mind, therefore, there is no form, no sound, no smell, no taste, no object of touch, no object of knowledge,

no more than there are domains of extension of the senses.

In fact, it is the same to say there is no seeing, no hearing, no smelling, no tasting, no touching, no perception of mental impression.

There is no visual consciousness, no auditory consciousness, no olfactory consciousness, no gustatory consciousness, no tactile consciousness, and no mental consciousness.

1. Dharma: Sanskrit term with various meanings. It is derived from the Indo-European root DHR, which indicates the notion of base and support. Its two main meanings are:
- spiritual path in general and more particularly the one taught by the Buddha. In this sense, the word is often made more precise by the addition of the adjective holy or genuine.
- all the objects of knowledge, all that is existing. The term in this case is generally plural. It is often translated as phenomena.

2. Prince Siddhartha, before he was Shakyamuni Buddha, spent several years as a homeless monk after having left his father's palace. His wandering led him finally to the bank of the river Nairanjana, where he met five ascetics. For six years, he led an austere life in their company in the forest of Uruvilla. The river and the location of these austerities, near Bodhgaya, remain places of pilgrimage today. The Buddha, finally, ate only one grain of rice a day. His body was emaciated, his face was gaunt, his ribs were poking out, and his eye-sockets were hollow. However, he began to notice that these mortifications were of no help to his spiritual progress. On the contrary, the great weakness of his body translated as a weakness of the mind. He resolved to give up this extreme path and to regain some energy. First, he went to bathe in the river, but on his return, he was so weak that he collapsed to the ground and his five companions believed him to be dead. A young shepherdess, Sujata, came to the riverbank and, approaching the monk, she saw that he was still breathing. She offered him some milk and rice. The future Buddha accepted them and recovered the lucidity of his mind and his physical strength. Witnessing the scene, his five companions believed he was rejecting his goal and was returning to mundane life. They turned away from him with disdain.

Then, he went to the bodhi tree, where he attained perfect awakening. Initially, he thought it would be wiser not to teach human beings the path to the ultimate goal because he thought they would be incapable of understanding it. It was only after seven days of silence, that he answered the pressing request of Brahma and other gods of vedic India, and consented to teach. First, he resolved to show the path of truth to those who were his companions for six years of austerity. He found them at Deer

Park in Benares. When they saw him coming, the five ascetics resolved not to greet him or show any hint of esteem, continuing to see him as a renegade who had returned to mundane life. However, when the Buddha approached, the supernatural dignity emanating from him forced them to stand up and greet him with respect. The Buddha taught them the path, and they became his first five disciples.

3. The four noble truths form the heart of the first cycle of teachings given by the Buddha. The are:
- the truth of suffering
- the truth of origin of suffering
- the truth of cessation of suffering
- the truth of the path

The explanation of these Four Noble Truths is given in the second part of Bokar Rinpoche's teachings (page 39).

4. The ten negative or unwholesome acts are killing, stealing, sexual misconduct, lying, creating discord, using harsh words, meaningless talk, envy, ill will, and wrong view.

Part II

Prajnaparamita is the sword that cuts the link; the link is the grasping by the mind of phenomena as permanent. Although nothing like this exists, although all phenomena are lacking permanence, our mind remains prisoner of this conception; only Transcendent Wisdom can cut this conception at the root itself.

Seated as we are in this room, nothing hinders us, nothing fetters us, we are free. But that which appears true from the outside is no longer true if we consider our mind. Our mind is bound, it seems inescapably. And from the absence of freedom of the mind, our suffering is born. Illusions follow karma; these illusions produced by conflicting emotions are like darkness covering our mind, and Transcendent Wisdom is the rising sun dissipating all obscuration.

This quality of Transcendent Wisdom is really that which is indispensable to us. Not having it, we are lacking an essential, vital element. We saw in the first part of this lecture that all beings having a mind are prisoners of certain perceptions and spontaneous graspings:

- grasping of the I
- grasping of permanence
- grasping of phenomena as potentially pleasant
- grasping of phenomena as pure

We also saw how spontaneous perceptions within the limitations of the cycle of conditioned existence, or relative reality, have some appearance of reality. However, we also saw how, in the light of the teachings of the dharma, when one ceases to consider things through a purely mundane analytical method, all this disappears and loses its reality. We saw how this me, the I that we automatically accept as evident appears, when we submit it to detailed examination, to be, instead of our usual monolith, a composite of five aggregates: form, feeling, perception, mental formation, and consciousness. We also have seen, by a precise and analytical examination of these five aggregates, that we can show their lack of intrinsic existence. We saw that the elements that compose the me are extremely disparate and have no existence on their own. This I/me that we never question does not have an existence in itself. We examined the notion of permanence and continuity, and we became aware that the outer world, as well as the beings it contains, was lacking stability. In fact, that which we consider continual and permanent actually changes from instant to instant and constantly passes. What is past no longer exists, that which is future does not exist yet, and the present is a mere hypothetical transition between the past and future. By this fact, the phenomena we consider are nevertheless the most immovable; they have no real and permanent existence. The house built today inevitably will become a ruin, and this process of decay and destruction began at the instant the house was achieved.

At some time, it will be a new house; then, imperceptibly, it will become an old house, even without us noticing it. Finally, sometime later, it will fall into ruin. This process of aging is continuous. The house changes from instant to instant, unceasingly. In the same manner, at our birth, our body was radically different from the adult body that will be ours and represented only a part of its present size and weight. However, no one can pinpoint the very moment it became adult or when the body found its definitive size. It is a slow process that has unfolded since childhood, imperceptibly, unceasingly, from instant to instant. This process will continue until we become old, without knowing how and when old age has begun for us. It is likewise for the constant passage of time. Day passes from morning to night, from hour to hour, from instant to instant in an uninterrupted flow that we cannot directly grasp. Of course, we may affirm the existence of a past, a future, and a present. However, we cannot take hold of this present. The minuscule moment of a finger snap is infinitely divisible. In fact, what we call present is something impossible to find or grasp. It is the same for pleasure and suffering. If we examine them, if we try to grasp their reality, we become aware that they are without self-existence.

In the same manner, the notion of pure and impure being—although instinctive and, for some of its aspects, innate—turns out to be completely illusory after examination. No phenomenon can be called pure or impure in itself.

There is no ignorance, no cessation of ignorance, and so on up to no old age and death, no cessation of old age and death.

We have seen the lack of own existence of the different constituents of the I, and in particular, of the five aggregates. We have seen that this I was emptiness, and that emptiness was not to be found elsewhere. Now the text affirms that there is no ignorance (marik pa, Tibetan; Avidya, Sanskrit).

1. This ignorance, nevertheless, is at the root itself of the twelve interdependent links, it is the first of them. It is the origin, the beginning, the source of appearance of all suffering in the cycle of existence. However, this ignorance does not cover or veil our mind. The own nature of our mind is emptiness, free of any characteristics. The nonrecognition of this fundamental mode of the mind is called ignorance (*avidya*). At our level, it manifests crudely, verifying that we are constitutionally unable to see from where we came and to where we are going. Where do beings come from? Where do they go? What are the causes of suffering or joy? And so on. We are unable to see all these phenomena directly. It is only from this fundamental ignorance that the concept of an I can appear.

2. The second of these interdependent links is mental formation.

3. From mental formation appears the individual consciousness.

4. Individual consciousness allows the manifestation of nama-rupa, name and form.

5. Faculties of perception are organized in visual, olfactory, gustatory, tactile, auditory and mental senses.

6. Contact can happen; contact is the meeting between an object considered as outer and the sense organ.

7. This contact produces pleasant, unpleasant, or neutral feeling.

8. Feeling engenders craving, a desire to make this feeling last.

9. Craving culminates in grasping; that is, one takes over this feeling, identifies with it, and tries to repeat it.

10. From this grasping, becoming occurs; becoming finds its full expression in the so-called three worlds.

11. Becoming ends in birth, which, for us, translates as obtaining a body.

12. Birth causes the appearance of old age, which finds its accomplishment in death, ending the cycle of the twelve interdependent links.

The cycle of existence manifests following the mode of the twelve interdependent links, which have their roots, their origin—not with a temporal meaning, but rather as base for appearance—in ignorance. These twelve links are called interdependent because one link cannot exist without the others. The necessary condition for the appearance of these links is the existence of the other ones. One could believe that it is because these twelve links are real that the cycle of existence can manifest. That is not correct, however. These twelve links appear only as a manifestation of the mind that functions in an illusory mode.

How does it happen then that samsara manifests? In fact, phenomena can manifest, appearing as reality without requiring a real base. This is illustrated by the classic example of a dream. We can dream of a complete existence with its experiences. When we awaken, we become aware that that complete existence was only an illusion, with no real base unfolding outside in the so-called real world. What is valid for the dream is also valid for the reality when we awake.

We see that the twelve interdependent links and the cycle of existence find their origin in ignorance. But this ignorance itself is without own existence. That is affirmed in the text, there is no ignorance (Tibetan, ma rik pa me). This affirmation refers to the level of ultimate reality where, in effect, ignorance does not exist. At the level of relative reality, however, it exists.

If, therefore, there was no ignorance, no manifestation of karmic tendencies or formations would appear, and by this fact, neither would consciousness, feeling, or any one of the subsequent links. By the fact that this first origin, which is ignorance, does not exist, the twelve interdependent links have no existence. It is what is expressed in the words, there is no ignorance. In summary, it is the negation of the twelve interdependent links as we listed them.

Since there is no ignorance, there is no cessation of ignorance, because something that does not exist cannot cease.

Likewise, there is no suffering, no origin of suffering, no cessation of suffering, no path.

In the same way that there is no cessation of ignorance, there is no cessation of any of the twelve interdependent links. There is no suffering, origin of suffering, or cessation of suffering; nor is there a path that leads to this cessation. It is the negation of the Four Noble Truths, or more precisely, the affirmation of their nonexistence.

- The first of these Noble Truths, the Truth of suffering, affirms and shows that as long as a being stays prisoner in the cycle of existence, his or her entire existence is suffering. However, for the same reasons, this suffering does not really exist. It does not have an existence on its own.

- The origin (kun jung) of suffering is karma and conflicting emotions. Using the same precedent, one shows the nonexistence of the origin of suffering. There is no origin of suffering.

- The path is made up of an assortment of means that allows us to go beyond suffering and causes suffering to cease. This is true on the level of relative reality, as long as one has not realized *Prajnaparamita*. But from the moment one has attained Transcendent Wisdom, the path no longer exists; it is no longer necessary.

- In fact, the goal of the path is cessation, the cessation of suffering that is obtained by realization of the true nature of the mind. This goal exists only as long as one lies buried in relative reality. From the very moment that one has done what was necessary to obtain the goal, from the actual moment one realizes Transcendent Wisdom, the goal ceases to exist.

There is no primordial awareness, no accomplishment, and no nonaccomplishment.

We try to travel over the path that leads to Awakening and obtain as the fruit of this path, Buddhahood, or Awakening which is first of all, supreme knowledge. But at the very instant we attain the goal, we realize that supreme knowledge also is lacking an existence on its own.

Tob pa me, there is nothing to obtain.

As long as we are buried in relative reality, we go searching for Awakening, Liberation, or Buddhahood, but once Transcendent Wisdom is realized, we become aware that there is nothing to obtain.

Ma tob pa yang me to, there is no nonobtaining.

It is important to understand at which level this teaching is placed. It is an ultimate teaching, that is to say, a representation—that can only be negative—of the phenomena as they appear when one perceives them in their true nature (suchness). This describes reality as perceived by someone who has already realized Transcendent Wisdom. We, ordinary beings, stay attached to the concepts of path, wisdom, obtaining, and goal to attain, and we act in function of these concepts. But, when one arrives at realization of the true nature of the mind, at Transcendent Wisdom, there is nothing to negate or to reject. Simply, everything falls down by itself, and we realize that it does not exist. There is no suppression of something that never existed in the first place.

Therefore, Shariputra, since these bodhisattvas have nothing to attain...

Effectively, bodhisattvas have nothing to obtain because their realization relies on this Transcendent Wisdom which has no goal to be attained.

Their mind being without veil, they have no fear. Fear appears from a false vision of reality. This false vision being nonexistent, fear cannot appear. This total absence of fear is a consequence of perfect realization. All that was said in the Heart Sutra of Transcendent Wisdom happens when a being who grasps as existing the five aggregates, the twelve interdependent links, the eighteen elements of senses, little by little trains to apprehend them as illusory. This being arrives, then, at the realization of Transcendent Wisdom, where they really are perceived as not existing.

Because of this process, all the Buddhas of the past have obtained the state of perfect Buddhahood. It is like this for those who obtain it now.

All the Buddhas manifesting in the three times, it is also by leaving it up to Profound Transcendent Wisdom that they effectively have attained the perfectly realized Buddhahood.

Therefore, the heart itself of this Transcendent Wisdom is the mantra of transcendent wisdom.

It is the mantra of the great knowledge.

By realization of this Transcendent Wisdom, one perceives the true mode of all phenomena, dissipating all ignorance. It is, therefore, the mantra of great knowledge, opposing great ignorance.

As an expression of Transcendent Wisdom, it is beyond all wisdom. It is the unsurpassable mantra which expresses the ultimate mode of phenomena.

It is the mantra that equals the unequaled.

A being submitted to the illusory mode of functioning of the mind perceives phenomena as good, bad, pure, impure, and so on. He or she discriminates phenomena and classifies them with a scale of values. Realization of Transcendent Wisdom recalls all phenomena to the absence of their own existence, and therefore, they are all perfectly equal.

It is the mantra that perfectly dissipates all suffering.

As it was seen, when one realizes Transcendent Wisdom, suffering itself is perceived as having no existence.

In truth, without lying, it is really like that.

It is the word of the Buddha, therefore perfectly pure and without error.

The mantra of the Perfection of Transcendent Wisdom is said like this: Tayata Om Gate Gate Paragate Parasamgate Bodhi Soha.

Tayata: Thus

Om: Primordial sound that begins mantras

Gate: Gone

Gate, Gate, Paragate: Gone, gone, gone beyond

Parasamgate: Perfectly completely gone beyond

Bodhi Soha: To Awakening.

The meaning of the utterance of the *Prajnaparamita* is entirely contained in this mantra. Avalokiteshvara then addresses Shariputra:

In the future, Shariputra, the bodhisattvas should train like this to acquire this Transcendent Wisdom.

Arising from his profound samadhi, the Buddha says, "Good, good, O son of noble family, in truth this is very good. Like this, the training of the realization of Transcendent Wisdom should be practiced. Thus, it has to be done as you have said."

All the Tathagatas (Buddhas) rejoice in the clear exposition of Transcendent Wisdom.

The Baghavat having spoken, Shariputra, the noble Avalokiteshvara, all those who were in the assembly, gods, humans, nonhumans, gandharvas, and all the beings in the cycle of existence, recognized the reality of that which was said.

This concludes the brief explanation of the Heart Sutra of Transcendent Wisdom.

The essence of this teaching is concentrated in the fact of considering the I, ego, as nonexisting and of conceiving of the five aggregates, the twelve interdependent links, the eighteen elements, and all phenomena *without exception* as emptiness.

However, one should not confuse emptiness and empty with nothing-at-all and nothingness. This teaching shows emptiness of all phenomena, in order to fight the innate tendency to grasp the I as really existing, as well as grasping material phenomena as permanent. This natural tendency, which does not need to be developed, consists of grasping the universe that surrounds us and ourselves as really existing. By the realization of Transcendent Wisdom, we can dissipate the suffering in the cycle of existence as well as the illusory appearances stemming from egocentric grasping.

The text of *Prajnaparamita* belongs to the second cycle of the teachings of the Buddha. There is a third one, which was transmitted not in a definite place but in diverse places to bodhisattvas whose understanding was particularly broad. In the latter teaching, it is said that all phenomena are **Tro pa dang drel wa**, that is, free of production, diffusion, and characteristics. Phenomena are beyond the characteristic of empty or not empty, having or not having an own existence.

During the first cycle of teachings, we have seen that the Buddha began by defining that which one calls I and showed that this I was composed, in fact, of the five aggregates and eighteen sense elements. After this was established, he showed, in the second cycle of teaching, the emptiness and nonexistence of these five aggregates, eighteen elements, and twelve interdependent links. Apprehending phenomena as emptiness effectively allows the cessation of all suffering and the cycle of existence. However, one problem remains: the grasping of emptiness as such. When one grasps emptiness as existing, "it is emptiness," it is a concept and, by this very fact, it is not really Transcendent Wisdom. This is why there is a third cycle of the teachings showing that fundamental reality is beyond any concept and point of view. It is beyond being and not being, emptiness and nonemptiness.

This mode of the *dharmakaya*, ultimate reality, is really beyond any concept. It is beyond being or not being, beyond the fact of neither being nor not being, beyond any logical possibility of conceptualization. Although this ultimate reality can be apprehended neither from the outside by the means of conceptual representation nor transmitted to another, it can, however, be experienced and realized from the inside. It will rise and appear in the mind. It is that which is expressed in the short praise that precedes the Heart Sutra.

Inexpressible and inconceivable Transcendent Wisdom
Not appearing, not ceasing, essence of space
You are perceivable only in the domain of the supreme knowledge,
I pay homage to you, mother of the Buddhas of the Three times.

This corresponds to ultimate realization. As long as we do not have this realization, we have no foundation to express ourselves in this manner. It cannot be intellectually understood, but it has to be experienced.

This is the reason for the three cycles of the teachings of the Buddha. Revealing *Prajnaparamita* is the heart of the second cycle of teaching, the *Mahayana*, as well as the ultimate realization of the *Vajrayana*. Although that which needs to be realized in these two vehicles is that all phenomena and *Prajnaparamita* have the same fundamental nature, *Vajrayana* is superior to *Mahayana* because it uses extremely efficient, powerful, and profound means that allow a swift realization of this ultimate meaning.

Concerning anger

We are born as human beings and have the qualities necessary for following a spiritual path. We know this. We have met with masters and have engaged on the path. Having these, we are very fortunate. We should know, however, that this human existence is not eternal. All phenomena are transitory. From instant to instant, all that is manifested is marked by impermanence. Before impermanence strikes our existence, before our death, it is essential to practice the Dharma. Our present life was prepared and conditioned by past lives. It is clear that those who are born now in the West were generous and accomplished many positive acts in their past lives. In this manner, they have accumulated a strong positive potential whose present actualization is an abundance of material goods, rich lands, more than enough food, comfortable houses, and so on. Nevertheless, the mind of Westerners knows suffering and difficulty. Only spiritual practice can keep us safe from this suffering. Modern science has produced wonderful inventions, all kinds of machines and apparatus, but none of them has the power to dissipate the deep suffering experienced by the mind. The path showed by the Buddha is the best means to eliminate suffering. That is why he taught it. The force of your positive potentiality now leads you to be interested in the dharma. It is important that the theoretical understanding you will have of the dharma is followed by regular practice.

The passions[1] that inhabit our mind are the main cause of our mental affliction. Among them, anger and aggressiveness are most particularly causes of suffering for us as well as for others. When they strongly arise in us, not only is our mind troubled, but we are no longer able to eat or sleep. The consequences to others are obvious: unkind words, insults, even physical violence, and murder.

An aggressive person constantly nourishes anger within himself or herself, creating an inner situation that is painful and distressing. Relationships with his or her environment, family, and friends can only be difficult. The atmosphere maintained by anger is a permanent source of tension. An angry person is not loved. Everyone strives to avoid him or her. This lack of affection and esteem brings the person frustration. An angry or hateful person can offer all kinds of gifts to people around him or her, but no one will be satisfied with them. One will have as little contact as possible with this kind of person.

Clearly, on the level of international relationships, aggressiveness is the main cause of wars, conflicts, and arguments. At the family level, anger is followed by disagreement, not getting along with others, and arguments.

Suffering produced by anger is not limited to present life. This suffering creates a karmic potential that will ripen in future lives, and its strength is enough to engender a type of hellish existence or, at least, much suffering.

We compare anger to an inferno. The water that puts out this inferno is the mind of awakening.[2] The mind of awakening is the remedy by which anger naturally dissipates. When present in our heart, this mind of awakening makes us happy, relaxed, and open. Happiness of our mind opens our heart to loving and comforting words, and our activity benefits others. When the mind is at peace, speech and body are also at peace and we are a balm for everyone.

Established in peace by the mind of awakening, we benefit not only our family, friends, and immediate entourage but also the country in which we live. If all human beings were inhabited by the mind of awakening, it is obvious that the whole world would know inner and material happiness.

Benefits of such loving behavior also surpass the framework of this life. Karmically, this behavior leads to obtaining an excellent existence as a human or deva[3] in the future.

It is true that in a natural way, anger is strongly anchored within us. We can, therefore, doubt that the mind of awakening might overcome it. We should not forget that the mind, whatever turn that we want to give to it, is very flexible. To the extent that we train ourselves, we create a habit and the mind accepts the crease that we give it. A field of study may at first seem very complex to us and even beyond our capabilities; however, regular effort will progressively assure us an understanding of what seemed impossible to grasp. In the same way, we can eliminate anger and aggressiveness from our mind and replace them with the mind of awakening. At first this task is difficult, but gradually it comes to fruition.

Internally, aggressiveness is similar to an adult in the full maturity of his or her age, while the mind of awakening is only a two- or three-year-old toddler. If we take care of nourishing this child, soon this child also will be an adult. At the same time, adult-aggressiveness will get old, losing strength and power. If we practice, the overthrow of these forces is possible. The mind of awakening, weak at the beginning, will increase as aggressiveness decreases.

UNDERSTANDING OTHERS

How can we develop the mind of awakening?

All beings, as we do, aspire to be happy and fear suffering. When we deeply understand this, we see the source of joy and happiness for us; it is also like that for others. We can decide right now to give others this happiness through our physical work, speech, or mind. Even if we are not able to effectively help others in the present, we still have the possibility of giving right orientation to our mind. This is done by cultivating the aspiration to find ourselves in a situation that will allow us to do so.

In a similar way, let us look at the effect of a hurtful word addressed to us, or an action through which one seeks to harm us. The sensitivity of all beings is the same;

just as we suffer, others do also. Therefore, we can understand the necessity for putting aside the part of our activity, speech, and mind that can engender suffering within others. If it is impossible for us to immediately give up some aspects of our conduct, at least we can aspire that they will disappear sometime in the future. To keep an attitude oriented toward benefiting others within our heart is what we call the mind of awakening.

RESPONDING TO AGGRESSIVENESS

We might act in a beneficial way, but it may happen that a person holds back or develops a negative attitude toward us. For ourselves, the right answer will be to feel compassion for this person. We think, "This person does not know the mind of awakening. Carried away by anger, this person speaks to me with anger, aspires to harm me, and is not in control of self." A mother might have a child who is made aggressive by mental illness. This mother does not condemn her child. She knows the child's behavior is caused by sickness. In facing aggressiveness, she answers with love. In a similar way, the person who returns good with harmful actions is the slave of the tendencies of his or her mind. Compassion is the only correct way to deal with this situation.

The mind of awakening loves and wants to help each and every being. It considers each and every being as a friend without exception.

Today, skillful surgeons can remove an organ that no longer functions and replace it with a healthy organ. This is useful for the body, but the person will be limited anyway to eighty or one hundred years at best. After that, the transplanted organ will not be of any use. Our mind also has a serious sickness of aggressiveness and anger. It is necessary to remove it in order to transplant, in its place, the mind of awakening. It is urgent surgery. Without it, not only will anger cause gangrene in our mind in this very life, but it will continue to affect our mind in future lives. Removing anger and transplanting the mind of awakening create, on the contrary, conditions of genuine happiness in this life and the lives to come. Under these circumstances, the surgeon is the perfectly awakened being, the Buddha, and the instructions on development of the mind of awakening serve as a scalpel.

Anger makes us stupid. Under the influence of anger, one sees couples fighting, tearing one another to pieces. Anger even creates situations leading to suicide. The mind loses control. On the contrary, the mind of awakening engenders peace and communicates happiness.

THE SIX PERFECTIONS

To cultivate the mind of awakening, we can lean on the bodhisattva's vows.[4] They are received from a lama, and each time anger rises in us, the strength of the commitment helps us avoid surrendering to its power. The bodhisattva's vows also imply complete development of our personality in the orientation of the mind toward awakening for the benefit of others. This is codified under the form of the six transcendent perfections (*paramita*, Sanskrit).

The first perfection is giving. It is most often divided in three parts, giving of material goods, giving of security, and giving of the spiritual path. Giving, be it only a crumb of food to a small insect, and doing it with a loving heart, is the perfection of giving. One should develop the habit of continually giving with this mind set.

The second perfection is ethics. In a general way, ethics consists of avoiding all that can harm others through our body, our speech, and our mind. Particularly, it takes the form of keeping the vows, whether they are monk, nun, or lay people vows.

Patience, the third perfection, consists of no longer reacting with anger to hurting words or aggressiveness directed against us. On the contrary, we answer with love and compassion. We often think that it is impossible to develop perfect patience; however, if we know our nature and our qualities, and if we train ourselves in them, it is completely possible to do it.

When someone reprimands us or addresses us with unpleasant words, anger naturally rises within us. If, however, we examine the nature of these words, we cannot find any substance in them. They are fundamentally only a series of articulated sounds, empty in essence. Reflecting in this way allows us to understand the uselessness of anger, which is not directed against something real. It is only founded on false apprehension of a phenomenon. Then, why maintain it?

If, on the other hand, we react with anger to a person who seeks to harm us, let us understand that this person cannot do anything else. His or her acts are not free. Let us suppose that someone threw a stone at me or hit me with a stick. Where does the pain that I feel come from? Without any doubt, from the stone or the stick. Should I then become angry at the stone or stick? Obviously not, because they have no responsibility. They are instruments of the hand that threw them. Am I going to get angry at the hand? Neither does it have any freedom because it is commanded by the person's mind. I must then rise up against this mind, but in fact this mind is not free, it is under the influence of anger. Anger is the root of this entire process. The person is not the master of the situation, and there is no reason why I should be angry with him or her. This type of reasoning helps considerably in cultivating patience.

The fourth perfection is diligence. Practicing the spiritual path and developing the mind of awakening require us to have no fear of failing any task, to be equal to the situation. They also demand persevering and regular training in meditation and the practice of positive acts. Continuity and dynamism on the path make up perfect diligence.

The fifth perfection is concentration. Our mind is usually inhabited by a crowd of thoughts. The mind itself is not free; it is the prisoner of these thoughts. The meditation called mental calming progressively takes the strength of thoughts and causes them to diminish. When the mind can be stabilized on the object of its choice, without distraction by any parasite thought, it is the perfection of concentration.

Then comes the sixth perfection, the perfection of wisdom. Now we identified ourselves with what we call the I, and are convinced of its real existence. The I is, nevertheless, an illusion. A person says my body, my arm, my leg, but it is not possible to discover the essence of the owner, because such a person has no own existence. Recognizing that the I exists only as a convention and not in essence is the perfection of wisdom.

Training in the six perfections in their totality does not happen in single day; it is rather a regular progress with no haste and discouragement. Training like this, we effectively practice the conduct of a bodhisattva. The six perfections are beneficial both for ourselves and for others. Giving, ethics, and patience are more geared toward others, while diligence, concentration, and wisdom primarily benefit ourselves.

Westerners have a high standard of living and possess material goods in abundance. However, they often hesitate on which path to take. In fact, the best path is the path of the bodhisattva. It brings happiness now and ultimately.

Benefits brought by this path are felt in the present, even if our capability to help others is very limited. However, this path ultimately leads us to awakening and buddhahood, which give us the possibility of benefiting others in unlimited ways.

QUESTIONS AND ANSWERS

Question: My dog is sick because of ticks. When I catch the ticks, I burn them. If I leave them, my dog is sick. However, I learned that one should not kill insects. What should I do?

Answer: The fact that your dog has parasites like ticks is the result of ripening of karma. Killing the ticks is a harmful act. Not killing them is allowing the dog to become sick. Each insect corresponds to a life. Each time one kills a single insect, one commits the act of suppressing life. If you feel compassion for them, you will not kill them. If however, you feel compassion for the dog, you will decide to relieve its suffering by killing the ticks. If you do so, recite the names of the Buddhas, mantras, and sacred wishes. This will help them for their future lives. It is up to you to decide for whom you have more compassion, for the ticks or for the dog, and to act accordingly.

Question: I try not to get angry at things or people, but I get angry with myself. When I am not successful in accomplishing something, I hit myself or hit the wall.

Answer: It is good to refrain from being angry with others, but it would be better not to become angry with yourself either. Anger at another person, or at yourself, is never a good quality. When you feel anger rising against yourself, think that it is a mistake and do not fall under its influence. Anger is always a defect. When it dominates us, we let ourselves say things that are extremely unpleasant and violent. Once anger is pacified, we see clearly that these words were out of proportion and stupid. It can happen that anger leads us to physical violence, for which we condemn ourselves later. It is the same toward ourselves. Anger in either case is not justified. It is good to know how to recognize that we have made some mistakes but it is useless to be irritated at ourselves. It is much more useful to analyze in a lucid manner the reasons for our mistake, and consider how we can avoid this mistake if the same situation happens again.

Question: If we get angry with ourselves, what are the means to pacify us?
Answer: There are many means that can be used to dissipate anger with oneself or others.

The first one is to recall the defects of anger and the qualities of serenity.

The second means envisions the debt we have toward all beings. Without exception, all beings were our mother or our father during one of our past lives. Any person with whom I am angry or whom I reject momentarily, had the love and kindness of a father and mother for me. Consequently, hatred and anger can only be a mistake. Only love is the right answer.

A third way is to refer to the dream. In a dream, I can become angry with someone for one reason or another.

However, it is clear—and I know it when I wake up—that neither the anger nor the situation that engendered it had any real existence. In the waking state, it is the same. Submitting to illusion, we take for real what is not. When we see anger rising, we can think that we are making an error, we are mistaken. In fact, the anger and the situation are of the same nature as the dream, without any real existence.

A fourth means examines the essence of anger itself. In particular, when anger that seems irrepressible arises and is ready to drown us, we should examine what it truly is. Generally, we sense that anger exists in a substantial way, as a thing that would really be there. Let us see which matter it is? What color is it? Is it black, red, or yellow? Which shape is it? Is it oval, round, or squared? What size is it? Where does it dwell? In the head? In the heart? In the chest? It will be impossible to find a single thing that we could call anger. However, in the state of illusion which dominates us, we consider anger as existing, although it does not. We are certain of its reality.

Question: Can we consider anger a sickness? Some people are angrier than others.

Answer: We can look at anger as an illness. It is even the most serious sickness there is, more dangerous than a physical illness. A physical and incurable illness touches only the body and will last, at the longest, one hundred years. When the body dies, the physical sickness does not enter the body in the following life. Anger is a different matter, following us to our next rebirths. It is a painful ordeal for those carried away by it, as long as they have not uncovered its lack of reality using the kind of analysis we have just explained. In fact, anger and physical pain have something in common. When we examine them, we discover they have no real existence.

Everyone here feels some difficulties and inner suffering to a lesser or greater degree. Is this not true? You perceive this suffering as something really existing in itself, present in your heart as a thing. Most of this suffering comes from the past or the future. We think about past painful or unfortunate events, or we envision the future with worry and fear.

What is this suffering coming from the past? The past is gone. It no longer exists. However, we go looking for past events to which we attribute a false reality in the present, and by doing so, we suffer. It is a process completely similar to experiencing, in the present, a reality of supposed events of the future which have no existence at all, either.

We let a past that no longer exists and a future that does not yet exist cause us a lot of torments. If, on the contrary, we establish ourselves in the present, we will see that, in most cases, our suffering becomes blurred. In essence, suffering does not really exist.

Knowing how to keep a relaxed and happy mind, cultivating the mind of awakening at the same time, is certainly the best thing to do.

Question: What can we do when we physically suffer because of an accident or sickness?

Answer: Physical suffering experienced now is actualization of a karmic potential formed during our past lives. To rid ourselves of this negative karma, we must practice with the appropriate spiritual means. To rid ourselves of pain, we must take the prescribed medicine.

1. The word "passion" is used here in its classical sense, as is still used in religious and ascetic vocabulary. It means mental productions bringing trouble in the mind or obscuring it with anger, desire, jealousy, pride, apathy, and so on. The same term (*klesia*, Sanskrit; nyom mong pa, Tibetan) is also translated as conflicting or afflicting emotions.

2. Mind of Awakening (*bodhicitta*, Sanskrit) is the motivation to attain awakening for the benefit of others. It is composed of two aspects:

- ultimate: understanding of the ultimate nature of all phenomena

- relative: development of love and compassion.

This text mainly refers to the second aspect.

3. Devas, in the Indo-buddhist cosmology, are the highest class of beings in the cycle of conditioned existence. They are not awakened beings, but they enjoy an extremely long and happy life.

4. The term "bodhisattva" is a compound of two Sanskrit words, the latter offering an ambivalent meaning. Bodhi means Awakening and sattva can mean being or courageous, heroic. Tibetans, when they had to translate the Buddhist texts from India into their language, chose the second meaning, and they formed the term "Jangchub Sempa." This can be translated in English as hero of awakening or awakened warrior (as translated by Trungpa Rinpoche) or knight of awakening. The latter has within it, connotations of heroism and generosity in the service of an ideal. The bodhisattva is one who is ready to face the difficulties in his or her progress toward awakening, in order to benefit others. He or she is ready to give his or her own life, as the Buddha Shakyamuni did in one of his past lives when he offered himself as food to a tigress and her starving cubs. The bodhisattva is even ready to defer attaining perfect awakening if the delay would be beneficial to others.

In a broader sense, a bodhisattva is a person who takes the bodhisattva's vows—as a knight had to be dubbed—and tries to go further on the path of the six perfections. However, with a restricted meaning, the term is applied to those having taken these vows, and have already attained one of the ten levels of liberation, which are called the ten *bhumis* or bodhisattva grounds. Beyond these ten levels, the path reaches at its ultimate end, complete awakening, or buddhahood. Although they have not attained this ultimate state, the bodhisattvas of the ten levels are beings of very high spiritual accomplishment, free from the links of the cycle of conditioned existence, and endowed with qualities and powers out of reach of a common being. For instance, they may appear as human beings in the domain of ordinary manifestation. They are then in the world but not of this world. They can also manifest in pure lands and have a body of light. The possibilities of manifestation of a bodhisattva being multiple, their simultaneous presence in different worlds is not contradictory.

The bodhisattva's vows can be taken by any ordinary being. They are the formal commitment enunciated in front of the Buddhas and bodhisattvas to move toward awakening in order to benefit others. This commitment implies practicing the six perfections, not surrendering to discouragement, and not withholding from any being the range of our compassion. These are the specific vows of the Great Vehicle (*Mahayana*).

Karma

Khenpo Donyo

ORIGIN OF THE WORLD

The original causes of the manifested world have been interpreted differently by various religions, traditions, and philosophies. Some people look at the universe as the creation of a superior god. For Hindus, it is Brahma or Vishnu; for others, another god or a unique god. There are philosophies that, on the contrary, envision the phenomenal world and its evolution as the result of random creation, without the intervention of any outside, intelligent agent. Buddhism has adopted another point of view. The production of appearances, whether they cause happiness or suffering, is due to what is called karma. This diversity of opinions leads us to wonder about their value.

Presenting all manifestation as the creation of a superior god who judges the acts of creatures is certainly a good thing. This belief stresses the necessity of adopting positive behavior to be accepted in heaven, and refraining from negative acts to avoid being thrown into hell. In this way, we are encouraged to discriminate and choose the right mode of living. Although useful, this presentation does not correspond to the strict truth from the point of view of the Buddhist teachings. In the teachings of the

Buddha, the world is not the creation of a superior being, of Buddha, Shiva, Vishnu, or anyone else.

The way of thinking that considers the universe as the result of random creation, without the intervention of an intelligent cause, is, at the opposite, a very harmful system. Living with this idea effectively implies that there are no long-term positive or negative acts outside the framework of this life, because these acts are neither submitted to a divine retribution nor do they have karmic consequences. One is, therefore, justified to act as one wishes, without any concern other than the laws of society in which one lives. This way of looking at things has the additional risk of allowing the distraught person to face suffering alone and notice its absurdity. There is no superior reality in which to place hope and find help. Physical suffering can be relieved by medical remedies, but there is no relief for inner turmoil.

The theory of karma is in itself the foundation of the teachings of the Buddha. When we are convinced of its validity and understand its functioning, we can consider ourselves to be effectively following the path of the Buddha. In Tibetan, the short expression of the translated Sanskrit word "karma" is formed with two syllables, *lay dray*. The first one, *lay*, means acts, and the second one, *dray*, results. In fact, these two syllables hide numerous implications, and it is difficult to expose the details and their network of interrelations. The principle of the karmic law is, nevertheless, easy to understand. Certain types of acts, by necessity, are followed by certain kinds of results.

This is the meaning of the elliptic expression, acts-results. A positive activity in this life will engender pleasant conditions of existence in future lives, and negative activity painful conditions of existence. Similarly, the happiness and suffering we encounter now are fruits of positive or negative acts accomplished in past lives. All manifestation of phenomena is due to karmic productions of the beings who experience it.

Some persons, contemplating this theory, believe that the Buddha was, above all, a very skillful leader in the human world. To have discipline reign through kindness in the ranks of his disciples, did he make up this fable? A fable accepted by simple people who would live in accord with right conduct leading to happiness? People convinced that incorrect conduct leads to unhappiness? And all his brave disciples behaved! It is obvious that the Buddha did not possess such contingent motivations, skillful as they are. What he expressed was nothing other than functioning of the karmic law as it is. He did not make up anything. He described what he saw with the perfect realization of his direct experience.

RESPONSIBILITY

Understanding how the law of karma functions places us in a relatively comfortable situation in the face of suffering and joy. Struck by suffering, we endure it without revolt, knowing it is the result of our karma. We, ourselves, have created the seed in our past lives. We are responsible for it. This attitude, in itself, diminishes suffering. When, on the contrary, we are in good times, we recognize similarly that this, too, is the fruit of acts in our past lives. Consequently, we do not look at ourselves as favored by fate, elected by gods, or blessed by fairies, being privileged, and benefiting from a distinguished destiny. We then avoid pride and conceit.

INESCAPABILITY

Karma is a law, and, as such, it is inescapable. A certain type of act is necessarily followed by a certain type of result. Before this life, we had other lives. Not a number that can be ascertained but an infinite number of lives. In effect, we cannot say we had begun to exist at a precise moment, and that before that moment we were not existing. This would be saying beings appear from nothingness, which is a contradiction in terms. During countless past existences, we accomplished countless acts; some were of a positive nature, and some of a negative nature. The karmic results of a number of them have already been experienced, but a large portion of them remains in potential state and will, of necessity, have to be experienced later. This inescapable characteristic of karma completely confronts us with our own responsibility. No acts of ours are without consequences.

INDIVIDUAL KARMA AND COLLECTIVE KARMA

We can distinguish two types of karma, individual and collective karma. The latter, however, does not cancel individual responsibility at all. Individual karma refers to acts that I have accomplished alone and, consequently, I will be the only one to experience the results. Collective karma designates acts accomplished in common by a group of people who will harvest the fruits together. Everyone who provoked the cause will experience the result, but both cause and result have collective characteristics. For example, a plane crashes, causing the simultaneous death of four hundred people. The fact that these violent deaths are a common fate indicates there was initially a common karmic cause. Even for less extreme occurrences, the connections we have with other people, the meetings we have attended, and the way we interpret them, depend also on strong or weak karmic relationships established in our past lives. Here again, we find common karma. I, myself, Khenpo Donyo, am an Easterner and you are Westerners. It happens that today, we have met. I came to talk to you, you came to listen. The only reason why this connection is possible is because of certain common karma in our past lives. The manner in which you perceive me depends also on this past karma. It is probable that some of you have immediately formed a favorable feeling toward me; some others have an unfavorable opinion. Some of you will find what I say very interesting, while some others will consider me boring and wordy. These different perceptions depend on our past karmic links.

Our karmic reservoir is a blend of positive and negative potentialities in varied proportions, depending on the individual. The law of karma is inescapable. When the negative part of our potentiality ripens, it will be experienced in the form of suffering. However, this inescapability is only true if other causes, able to modify the initial cause, do not happen. This is why, by using appropriate spiritual means, it is possible to rid ourselves of negative potentialities. The seed of a bad weed, lying dormant in the ground, will inescapably grow if we do nothing to hinder the process. If, however, we use a weed-killer or pull it out as soon as it begins to grow, its harmful characteristics will be neutralized. Our negative potential karma is similar to this seed. If we let it develop, it inescapably will actualize, but it is possible to neutralize it.

POSITIVE KARMA—NEGATIVE KARMA

Body, speech, and mind are all implicated in the production of positive as well as negative karma. Traditionally, one gives a list of the ten negative acts that are divided as follows:

- Three negative acts of the body: killing, stealing, and sexual misbehavior. The latter, for the most part, concerns monks and nuns bound by chastity vows.

- Four negative acts of speech: lying, creating discord by misusing language, addressing harmful words to someone, and engaging in futile conversations.

- Three negative acts of the mind: covetousness, ill-thinking and having erroneous conceptions about the true nature of phenomena.

Positive acts are opposite of these negative aspects. The first level consists simply in giving up negative acts. The second level is for us to exercise their opposite:

- for the body: protecting life, being generous, and respecting one's vows.

- for speech: saying the truth, reconciling people who do not get along, talking in a pleasant manner, and having right conversations.

- for the mind: cultivating contentment, developing kindness, having right views, especially being convinced of the validity of karma, the existence of the three Jewels,[1] and understanding the profound meaning of emptiness.

These different acts have specific consequences, so specific that it is really possible to have an idea of the past lives of people by observing the dominant characteristics of their present life, which is the ripening of past positive or negative acts. A long life indicates that the person protected life in his or her past existences; a short life is, on the contrary, the characteristic of those who suppressed life. Abundance of material goods indicates a past generosity; great poverty shows past stealing and dishonest appropriations. Physical beauty is the fruit of purely observed ethics, ugliness results from breaking chastity vows. Some people have the knack of expressing themselves. They are listened to by others and are well understood; having told the truth is the cause of this.

Others, even if they speak the truth are not believed or taken seriously. This indicates lying in past lives.

ACT AND MOTIVATION

Activity is not the only factor involved in the production of karma. Motivation is an essential factor that conditions the strength of karma. If, for example, moved by hatred, we kill an animal, even more a human, this motivation is extremely negative and will be followed by all the more painful results. It is said that, in this case, the result can be birth in the hell realm.[2] Our motivation to kill is not always hatred. It can be an entertainment for a hunter, or it can be just to get rid of some harmful insects. The act is negative, but the karmic consequences will be less serious and will result in only birth in the form of hungry ghost or animal.

Some people express reserve regarding the law of karma. They say facts seem to contradict it. Do we not see people kill, steal, and make others suffer; yet, these people maintain good health, have wealth, and are surrounded by friends? Do we not see kind, helpful, and loving people who are poor, ill, and overwhelmed by fate? Even though we are told that negative acts are followed by suffering and positive acts by happiness? So why is this? We are forgetting that generally karma does not ripen in one lifetime, but from one life to another, or even several lives after the act was committed. We can harvest, in this life, fruits of a good karma from our past lives, while at the same time creating negative karma, which will ripen as suffering in lives to come. At the same time, those who are now suffering, notwithstanding a positive conduct, can rid themselves of a negative burden and accumulate positive potentiality.

Ripening of karma takes variable lengths of time. Some acts committed in this lifetime can see fruits in this very life. Other acts require a lifetime or several lives; others, thousands of lives. There can be no absolute rule for determining the duration of ripening.[3]

SIMILARITY OF RELATIONS

Acts we do and karmic fruits that we harvest are linked by obvious relationships of similarity. For example, as we have seen, protecting life will lead to enjoying a long life; being generous to living in abundance; telling the truth to being believed, and so on. The story of Nagarjuna's death is a good illustration of this fact.

Nagarjuna[4] was one of the great masters of ancient Buddhist India. His fame was so great that he was called the second Buddha. He was at this time the close friend of a king who had two sons. The older one was eager to ascend to the throne. Unfortunately for him, his aging father was not dying. The son was getting old, and he despaired of ever being able to realize his desire. He was beset with worry. He told his mother of his concern. She explained that there was, in fact, little hope because the king, and Nagarjuna had a common karma, sharing the same span of life. Nagarjuna, by his realization, had obtained physical immortality, which designates in fact an extremely long life. For the king to die, Nagarjuna had to die also, but this seemed impossible. The mother advised her son to see Nagarjuna and ask him to die. The prince went to him and made his request. He explained his wish to Nagarjuna and added, "You are a great bodhisattva who vowed to do anything for the benefit of others. To fulfill my wish, your death is necessary. If you do not want to die for me, you are not a true bodhisattva." Nagarjuna nodded, "Kill me, I am ready!" The prince took his sword and tried to decapitate Nagarjuna, but although he struck again and again, he could not hurt his victim. He tried to strangle him with a rope, but nothing worked. One after another, he tried all kinds of means without success. Nagarjuna himself was also sad. "I have accepted death for him, but he is unable to kill me." Being endowed with immortality, he could not die. By the power of meditation, he went back among his past lives to see if there was any act with unexhausted karmic consequence, allowing him to die. He saw that a great number of *kalpas* ago, he had mistakenly cut the neck of an ant with a blade of kusha grass.[5] Karmic results of this act had not yet ripened. This discovery made him feel better. He told the prince that he will be able to kill him simply by touching his neck with kusha grass. This was done.[6] The relation of similarity between the cause and consequence is obvious here.

PURIFICATION

Karmic potential can be only erased from the innermost depths of the unconsciousness in two ways. It either actualizes itself in a given situation, or one purifies oneself with the appropriate means. Except for these two cases, karmic potential remains intact.

During countless past lives we committed countless negative acts. It is certain that all karmic results have not yet been experienced. Consequently, a more or less important negative potential lies dormant within us. If we leave these virtualities as they are, one day or another, in this life or another, they will actualize in the form of suffering. It is inescapable. However, this potential can be neutralized. We can eliminate it, heavy as it is, through purification. In his youth, Milarepa learned black magic in order to obey his mother who sought revenge. He used it to create a storm that caused the death of several people and the destruction of a house and numerous birds were killed by hail. Later, understanding the gravity of this act and its karmic consequences, he wished to purify himself. He searched for a master, repented, regretted, submitted himself to numerous painful hardships, and meditated. In such a way, he was able to purify himself completely in the same lifetime in which he accomplished the negative acts. He also purified himself of the totality of the negative potential accumulated since time without beginning and attained perfect awakening.

INTERPRETATION OF THE WORLD

Karma not only rules the conditions of our existence, it also determines the manner in which we perceive our environment and the way we interpret our relationships with beings and things. It is well known, for example, that beauty is a subjective matter. This subjectivity reflects, in fact, people's karma. Without doubt, some people will find the small rug in front of us quite beautiful; others will show no interest in it. These differences in appreciation are particularly great in the field of art. For some, a painting by a certain master is wonderful and expresses many things, while others judge the same canvas inexpressive, trivial, even, frankly, ugly.

Karmic relationship links us to objects and determines our perception. If this were not the case, an object would be beautiful in itself, and everyone would find it beautiful. However, karmic conditionings in relation to phenomena can be much deeper than simple differences of appreciation. They can be followed by fundamentally different mental perceptions. It is said that what we call water is perceived completely differently by other classes of beings. For the *devas*, it is wonderful nectar; for the hungry ghosts, disgusting liquid pus. Essentially, it is the same element, but the positive karma of the *devas* makes them perceive it as nectar, the mixed karma of human beings makes us perceive it as water, while the negative karma of the hungry ghosts makes them perceive it as pus.

Relationships between people are ruled by similar laws. A girl will meet a boy and will find him handsome, pleasant, and endowed with all the best qualities. Other girls will find the same boy ordinary. This is well known. If karmic conditionings were not significant influences, all the girls would find the same boy handsome, attractive, and so on. This is not the case because a karmic link is necessary in order to be attracted to a person, or for two people to be attracted to each other. If this link is missing, feeling will not be established.

It is also a commonly shared experience to find pleasant a person that we meet for the very first time, while we immediately feel antipathy for another one. Nevertheless, others will feel differently when introduced to the same people. These reactions on the first contact are not rationally justified. They are the expression of good or bad karmic relationship pre-established in past lives.

Let us suppose that a group of people go to a place where they have never gone before. Some people will find the place pleasant, some even will wish to live there, while others will consider the place lacking charm, even sad or inhospitable. The place, however, is the same. As with a relationship between people, it is the nature of karmic links that conditions appreciation of the place.

This process can be applied also to our spiritual connections. The Vajrayana,[7] for example, establishes relationships with diverse forms of awakening called deities, through the means of initiations. When we undertake the practice of one of these deities, we may feel in a familiar setting. With another, we may have the impression of being in the presence of a stranger. It is the sign of a relationship already established or not established in a past life.

Any intelligent person who understands the law of karma and its implications should avoid any negative act and adopt purely positive behavior. Unfortunately, even a great determination is insufficient to sweep away all habits formed in ourselves since time without beginning. Unconscious imprints conditioning our mind are too deep to be erased in a single instant. A positive restructuring of our mind can only be a long-term task.

QUESTIONS AND ANSWERS

Question: Our lives proceed from one to another since time without beginning. Will they have an end?
Answer: Our conditioned existence (in samsara) can have an end, or, in different words, we can become awakened. This does not mean that it is an automatic process, but if we take the right path, it will lead us to liberation.

Question: Once Buddhahood is attained, can we see all our past acts?
Answer: Attaining Buddhahood implies that one is totally purified of his or her karmic potential, which has completely disappeared. A Buddha has no more remaining karma, and Awakening is not a karmic fruit. The positive counterpart of this purification is omniscience. Therefore, a Buddha knows what all his or her acts were in the totality of past lives, and also knows how he or she got rid of the imprints.

This knowledge can be applied to others, in the smallest detail. If a Buddha were in this room, he or she would know what karmic causes make some of us have brown, blond, or gray hair, or no hair at all!

Question: If one attains Buddhahood in this very life, do all appearances disappear instantaneously?

Answer: Awakening does not mean that appearances disappear; however, they lose all their harmful characteristics.

Question: What is the bardo?

Answer: The Tibetan word *bardo* simply means in between. This means that the end of this life and the beginning of the following one are not concomitant. They are separated by some period of time that gives place to a particular existential state.

Question: Are the appearances manifested in the bardo the production of our mind? Do they have any connection with our future rebirth?

Answer: Phenomena appearing in the *bardo* are extremely diverse, but they do not have an existence in themselves. They are nothing other than the productions of our own mind. In the period called the *bardo* of becoming, these productions are, effectively, in relation to our rebirth.

The manifestation of a man and a woman toward whom we feel attracted will signify rebirth as a human being. The manifestation of a being of great beauty will indicate rebirth as a *deva*, and so on. Whether appearances that manifest are pleasant or unpleasant does not change how one needs to correctly view them. What allows us to liberate ourselves from them is to recognize their nature or to be conscious that they are only the production of our mind. If we do not recognize them, they will attract us or repulse and scare us, and we will again be led to a certain type of conditioned existence.

Being conscious of the lack of reality in phenomena of the *bardo* is accessible only to one who has made preparation during his or her lifetime. How? Through familiarizing oneself from this time forward to consider appearances as having no reality in themselves and as being similar to dream phenomena.

Question: When we practice or study the dharma, we do not always know whether we are on the right path or not. How can we know this?

Answer: Results of your practice are themselves the sign of its validity. More love and compassion, a deeper knowledge of the nature of our mind, a growing trust in the dharma and the masters who teach it, a greater conviction of the truth of the law of karma—all these signs indicate that our practice is right. If, on the contrary, we are full of doubts and grasping of emotions does not diminish, it is probably the sign that some aspects of the path are misunderstood or not well practiced. It is then better to seek the advice of a lama.

1. The three Jewels are the Buddha, who is the perfectly awakened being; the Dharma, which is his teachings; and the Sangha, which is the community of those who follow these teachings, particularly those who already have attained a level of liberation. In Buddhism, the three Jewels express transcendence and its pure manifestation. This transcendence can be designated differently in other traditions without falling into the domain of erroneous conceptions. Error is to negate transcendence, whatever it is called.

2. Buddhist cosmology divides the totality of possible existences manifested into the multiple universes in six major classes, each having numerous divisions:

- *devas*, or gods, in a meaning close to the one of ancient mythology. They are not awakened beings, but beings enjoying a very long life and pleasure of the senses
- *asura* or titans, closely related to the *devas* but proud and aggressive
- humans
- animals
- *pretas* or hungry ghosts, who experience a type of very painful existence, continually tormented by hunger and thirst they cannot quench
- beings in the hell realm, submitted to all kinds of torments and tortures. Traditional texts describe these worlds as manifesting permanent aggressiveness by the environment: trees with leaves like razor blades, rivers of melting lava, demons inflicting all kinds of tortures, and so on. In psychological terms, one will be tempted to say that beings in the realm of hell suffer from an extreme form of paranoia that conditions all their perceptions of the world. The degree of reality of the hell realms is often questioned. From the ultimate point of view, they are part of the general picture of intrinsic nonreality of all phenomena, and therefore of all realms. They are the union of emptiness and manifestation, having the nature of a dream. It is the characteristic of illusion itself that they are grasped as having a substantial existence. One can say that, in some manner, hells are like a gigantic nightmare. Like a nightmare, they exist

nowhere. Like a nightmare, they are perceived as being extremely dangerous to the one who experiences them.

3. Notions of maturation of karma and similarity of results are well illustrated in the following, gently humorous story told by Kalu Rinpoche. At the time of the Buddha Shakyamuni, a young woman became pregnant. Nine months passed, then ten, then twelve without her giving birth. Not only that, she conceived again and the second child was born without the first one being delivered. She had a third and fourth child but the oldest was not given birth yet. Years went by, and the woman, who had carried her child in the womb for sixty years, saw death coming. She asked her family to open her belly as soon as she breathed for the last time, so the child would not be cremated with her on the funeral pyre. They saved the child but, because of his age, he was old and toothless. Quickly, he became a disciple of the Buddha and in one or two years, obtained the state of *arhat* or liberation.

The case was unique enough for the closest disciples of the Buddha to ask the karmic cause. The Buddha revealed its mystery.

Numerous *kalpas* in the past, two monks wandered and begged together. The older was the master, the younger the disciple. Both of them had great faith in the Buddha, who was living at that time. Their wandering led them to a city where a theater performed. The younger monk wanted to go to the theater, and tried to convince his elder to come with him. The master argued that it was against their monks' rules and that it was out of the question. The disciple insisted unsuccessfully. Anger overcame him, and he told his master that he could stay sixty years locked in his own jail but that he, nevertheless, would go to the performance. And he went.

The karmic consequences of an act are greater if the object concerned is more spiritually developed. Offering flowers to a Buddha allows for the storage of positive potential greater than that generated by offering flowers to ordinary beings. Bursting into anger in front of one's spiritual master is infinitely more serious than in doing so in front of an ordinary being.

The result of the young monk's anger was that he was born in hell for many *kalpas*. When his karma finally allowed him to take human birth again, because of the sixty years of jail to which he had compared the monastic life of his master, he stayed locked up in his mother's womb. Because he had great faith in the past Buddha, he became a disciple of the present Buddha and swiftly obtained liberation.

4. Eight Indian masters are considered to be the greatest doctors of Buddhism: Aryadeva, Vasubandhu, Dignaga, Dharmakirti, Gunaprabha and Sakyaprabha from the group called the Six Ornaments of this world. Nagarjuna and Asanga, held in higher esteem, are called the Two Sublime Ones.

The life span of Nagarjuna is subject to argument. The Tibetan chronology has him living four centuries after the Buddha's *parinirvana*, which means around the beginning of the common era. Western scholars are inclined to think that he lived in the second half of the second century. This question becomes still more complicated because of the existence of a second Nagarjuna, a tantric yogi and alchemist identified by Tibetans with the first Nagarjuna, although centuries separate them. Obviously, scholars refuse to do so. One can understand their refusal to accept a traditional record that states that Nagarjuna lived for 571 years. However, for Easterners, this is not beyond belief; they easily accept that realized yogis are not governed by the natural laws that rule the destiny of ordinary beings. Moreover, as one can see by the story of Nagarjuna's death as told by Khenpo Donyo, legend and history are, for Easterners, two domains that permeate each other.

Nagarjuna is, above all, known to have codified the *Madhyamika*, the middle way, the heart of the philosophy of *Mahayana*. He composed six fundamental treatises. It is he who, in other aspects, revealed the teachings of the *prajnaparamita*. Told by the Buddha, they had been kept up to that point by the *nagas*, half-human, half-snake beings living in underground realms. Nagarjuna disclosed the dharma to them, and in exchange, they gave him many presents, including the texts of the *prajnaparamita*. The first part of his name is due to his sojourn with the *nagas*. The second part comes from the fact that he was as skilled at spreading the *Mahayana* as Arjuna was at using his bow. (Arjuna is the famous archer of the Indian Mahabharata to whom Krishna reveals the Bhagavat-Gita.)

5. Kusha grass is a long-stemmed plant used by brahmans in some ceremonies. Buddhists attribute a sacred characteristic to it because the Buddha sat on a cushion made of this grass when he attained awakening in Bodhgaya.

6. The Tibetan historian Taranatha adds that then a voice was heard saying, "From this place I go to the Pure Land of Bliss, but later I will come back in this body." The prince fearing the power of immortality of Nagarjuna would reunite the body and head, carried the head far away. There a kind of spirit took the head and placed it on a big rock. The rock exploded, taking the shape of statues of five deities. Head and body themselves became stone, and it is said that they are progressively moving together. Originally, four leagues were between them, while at the time of Taranatha (seventeenth century) they were only one eighth of a league apart. When the two rocks join, they will become alive and Nagarjuna will again teach the dharma on earth.

7. The Vajrayana is the esoteric path in Buddhism. Confined in India to the secret world of the yogi, it is partially public in Tibet. Its characteristic is to know how to channel and use the network of spiritual energy that sustains any manifestation.

SMALL GLOSSARY

ACCUMULATION OF MERIT: Practice of positive *acts*, allowing us to store energy for the progression on the spiritual path. This accumulation of merit can be done through the practice of giving, making offerings, reciting *mantras*, visualizing deities, and so on.

ACCUMULATION OF WISDOM: Practice of understanding the empty nature of all phenomena.

ACT: Physical action as well as words or thoughts.
NEGATIVE ACT: All negative deeds that deliberately cause others to suffer, and leave an imprint of more suffering on our mind that will condition our experience and vision of the world. *POSITIVE ACT*: Following the law of *karma*, an *act* is positive when it creates happiness in us. *TEN NEGATIVE OR UNWHOLESOME ACTS*: Killing, stealing, sexual misconduct, lying, creating discord, using harsh words, meaningless talking, envy, ill will, and wrong views. *TEN POSITIVE ACTS*: Protecting life, giving, having an ethical conduct, talking truthfully, reconciling people, talking with gentleness, talking about meaningful things, being content, will to benefit other beings, and giving up wrong views.

AWAKENING: State of *Buddhahood*.

BARDO: The word *bardo* means intermediate state. If used without any other precision, it means the length of time between death and rebirth. Theoretically, it lasts forty-nine days. It can also designate limited periods of time known as the *six bardos*:
- *bardo* from birth to death (present life)

- *bardo* of dream
- *bardo* of concentration (meditation)
- *bardo* of the time of death (process of dying)
- *bardo* of the nature of the mind it-self (first part of time following death)
- *bardo* of becoming (second part of time following death)

BEINGS: There are six classes of *beings*: gods (*devas*), demigods, human beings, animals, hungry ghosts, and hell beings.

BHAGAVAT: Designates the Buddha, The Victorious One, who is endowed with all qualities and is beyond samsara.

BODHGAYA: Place in India (Bihar state) where Buddha Shakyamuni attained Awakening.

BODHICITTA: Aspiration to obtain *Awakening* in order to help all beings. *ABSOLUTE BODHICITTA* is the realization of emptiness of all phenomena. *RELATIVE BODHICITTA* refers to the practice of compassion and is divided in aspiration (limitless love, compassion, joy, and equanimity) and application (practice of the six perfections or *paramitas*).

BODHISATTVA: Being who follows the *bodhicitta* path and seeks to obtain *Awakening* not only for himself or herself but for the sake of all *beings*. An ordinary being who commits to practice *bodhicitta*. One who has attained *Awakening* and dwells in one of the ten stages of the *bodhisattvas*. A *bodhisattva* can be physically present in our world or abide in domains of more subtle manifestation.

BUDDHA NATURE: Potential of *Awakening* inherent in all *beings*.

BUDDHA: One who has awakened. A person, as the historical *Buddha Sakyamuni*. In Tibetan, *Sangyay*. *Sang* means purified from the conflicting emotions, duality and ignorance; *gyay* means that the infinite potential of qualities of a *being* is awakened.

BUDDHAHOOD: Awakened state characterized by wisdom (as knowledge of the true nature of phenomena and their manifestation in the *three times*), *compassion* for every *being* and power to help all *beings*.

CHENREZIG (Tibetan): Avalokitesvara (Sanskrit). *Buddha of Compassion*. Most popular Tibetan deity, his *mantra* is OM MA NI PAD ME HUNG. For more information, see *Chenrezig, Lord of Love*, published by ClearPoint Press.

CLARITY: With emptiness, one of the aspect of the nature of the *mind*. *Clarity* designates the dynamic aspect, which includes the faculty of knowing and creating all manifestation.

CLEAR LIGHT: Nature of the mind.

COMPASSION: Aspiration to liberate all *beings* from *suffering* and cause of *suffering*.

CONFLICTING EMOTIONS: Desire-attachment, hatred-aversion, ignorance or mental dullness, jealousy, pride, and so on.

CONSCIOUSNESS: From a dualistic point of view, each object of the senses corresponds to a consciousness. There are six or eight consciousnesses, depending on their classification. First, let us consider six consciousnesses:
- visual consciousness (forms)
- auditory consciousness (sounds)
- olfactory consciousness (smells)
- gustatory consciousness (tastes)
- tactile consciousness (tangible objects)
- mental consciousness (imaginary objects)
One can add two other consciousnesses:
- disturbed consciousness or ego consciousness, which corresponds to the influence of *conflicting emotions* on our relationship to phenomena
- potential of consciousness or "all-ground consciousness" (Sanskrit, alayavijnana), which contains all the latent conditionings of *karma*

DEDICATION: Aspiration that any merit accumulated through our positive *acts* serves to attain *Awakening* for the benefit of all *beings*.

DHARMA: *Buddha's* teachings or the spiritual path. *Dharmas* are phenomena.

EIGHTEEN ELEMENTS: Six sense objects (form, sound, smell, taste, tangible, and mental objects); six sense organs (eye, ear, nose, tongue, skin, and mind); six consciousnesses (visual, auditory, olfactory, gustatory, tactile, and mental) .

EMPTINESS: Fact that phenomena are devoid of independent existence, although they manifest.

FIVE AGGREGATES: Physical and mental constituents of a being prisoner of duality and illusion:
- aggregate of forms (physical elements and particularly the body)
- aggregate of feelings (pleasant, unpleasant, or neutral)
- aggregate of perceptions (understanding of the nature of that which produces pleasant, unpleasant, or neutral sensations)
- aggregate of mental formations (reactions toward perceived objects)
- aggregate of consciousnesses
At a pure level, these aggregates become the nature of the five *masculine Buddhas*.

FIVE ELEMENTS: Earth, water, fire, air, and space. They are the symbol of different states of the matter. Space designates the emptiness in which all manifestations appear. The essence of the five elements corresponds to the nature of the five *feminine Buddhas*.

FOUR NOBLE TRUTHS: They constitute the object of the first cycle of teaching given by the Buddha. They are the truth of suffering, truth of origination of suffering, truth of cessation, and truth of the path that leads to the cessation of suffering.

GIVING: There are three kinds of giving to others:
- material giving
- providing security
- making the *dharma* available

KAGYUPA: One of the four great schools of Tibetan Buddhism. The other ones are Gelugpa, Nyingma, and Sakya schools. The *Kagyu* lineage originates with Marpa the Translator in the 11th century.

KALPA: Cosmic era of extremely long duration.

KARMA: The law of *karma* describes the process of cause and effect. It is a three-phase process:
- An *act* leaves an imprint in the mind of the one who acts (cause).
- This *act* is stored in the potential of consciousness and is slowly ripening.
- This process is actualized in a particular form of *suffering* or joy (result).

LAMA (Tibetan): Guru (Sanskrit). A spiritual teacher.

LOVE: Aspiration to bring happiness to all *beings*.

MANTRA: Sacred sounds, the repetition of which helps the mind purify itself and develop its potential for *Awakening*. For example, the *mantra* of Chenrezig is OM MA NI PAD ME HUNG.

MAHAYANA: Vehicle of the bodhisattva, who aspire to attain awakening for the benefit of all beings.
MIND: This term can refer to the ordinary functioning of the *mind* called "psyche" as well as the absolute, nondual pure essence of the *mind* beyond the fluctuations that may affect the ordinary mind.

NIRVANA: Literally, extinguished, cessation. Early definitions included liberation from conditioned existence, ignorance, and conflicting emotions. Later definitions were expanded to include the development of great *compassion* through skillful means.

OBSCURATION: Conflicting emotions and dualistic perception that veil our *Buddha nature*.

OBSTACLES: Circumstances not favorable to the *dharma* practice, which can be experienced as external *obstacles*, internal *obstacles* (sickness), and secret *obstacles* (our own thoughts).

PARINIRVANA: Passing away of an awakened being or Buddha in order to teach impermanence to all beings.

PURIFICATION: All negative *acts* done in this life and in the past lives have left imprints in our potential of consciousness. These imprints will ripen, engendering *suffering* and *obstacles* to our spiritual practice. *Purification* will neutralize these imprints in order to avoid or reduce their effects. A qualified teacher might designate specific practice to do in order to purify oneself.

SHAKYAMUNI: Literally, "wise man of the Sakya," name of the historical *Buddha* who lived in the 6th century B.C.E.

SAMADHI: State of meditative concentration.

SAMSARA: Cycle of conditioned existence in which each *being* is born and dies. It is characterized by *suffering*, ignorance, impermanence, and illusion.

SANGHA: Community of Buddhist practitioners. One distinguishes ordinary *sangha* from the *Noble Sangha*, which is composed of those who have attained the *bodhisattva* levels.

SENDING AND TAKING: *Bodhicitta* practice of development of *love* and *compassion* through which one gives one's positive potential and happiness to others and takes their *suffering* upon oneself.

SIX SENSES: Visual, auditory, olfactory, gustatory, tactile, and mental senses.

SIX PERFECTIONS: (Sanskrit, *paramita*) Practiced on the *Mahayana* path, they are generosity, ethics, patience, diligence, concentration, and wisdom.

SUFFERING: Generally, it is analyzed on three levels:
- *suffering* of *suffering*: physical and mental pain experienced by all *beings*
- *suffering* of change: one experiences *suffering* when happiness ends
- *suffering* of conditioned existence: suffering one undergoes because of the deluded nature of *samsara*; it ends only when one attains *Awakening*.

SUFFERING OF THE HUMAN REALM: Birth, aging, sickness, death, sorrow, grief, despair, getting things we do not like, losing things we like, not getting what we wish for, and so on.

SUTRA (Sanskrit): Text of the exoteric teachings of the *Buddha*.

TAKING REFUGE: Placing oneself under the protection of the *Buddha, Dharma,* and *Sangha* (the Three Jewels). In the *Vajrayana,* one takes also *Refuge* in the Three Roots, *lamas, yidams* and dharma protectors.

TANTRA: Text of the esoteric teachings of the *Buddha,* which is related to a deity.

TATHAGATA:(Sanskrit) Name given to the *Buddha,* literally the one who is gone into suchness.

THREE JEWELS: The Buddhas, Dharma, and Sangha.

THREE TIMES: The past, present, and future.

THREE TURNINGS OF THE WHEEL: Classification of the Buddha's teachings. *The First Turning* of the Wheel of the Dharma was concerned with the Four Noble Truths, base of the Hinayana. It was taught by the *Buddha* at Deer Park, in Sarnath. *The Second Turning* of the Wheel was given on *Prajnaparamita* at Vulture Peak in the framework of the *Mahayana. The Third Turning* of the Wheel was concerned with the Heart Of Awakening and given at Vaishali. It is also part of the *Mahayana.*

TWELVE INTERDEPENDENT FACTORS OR LINKS: Ignorance, karmic formations, individual consciousness, name and form, six senses, contact, sensation, craving, grasping, becoming, birth, and old age and death.

VAJRAYANA: Path of Buddhism also called "Diamond vehicle" referring to the part of the *Buddha's* teachings written in texts of an esoteric nature called *tantras*. It uses recitation of *mantras, and visualizations* of deities and works with the *subtle winds* or energies.

VEILS: That which obscures our *Buddha nature* such as ignorance, latent conditioning, dualistic perception, *conflicting emotion, karmic* veils, and so on.

Index